Victorians

Published by Collins
An imprint of HarperCollins*Publishers*
77–85 Fulham Palace Road
Hammersmith
London
W6 8JB

**Browse the complete Collins catalogue at
www.collinseducation.com**

First published in 2006 by Folens Limited, as part of the *Folens Primary History* series.
Previously published as *A Time to Remember: Victorian Britain*.

10 9 8 7 6 5 4 3 2

ISBN: 978-0-00-746403-6

British Library Cataloguing in Publication Data
A catalogue record for this publication is available from the British Library.

Acknowledgements
The author and publisher wish to thank the following for permission to use copyright
material:
Aerofilms Limited, p5 (bottom right)
Architectural Association, p38
Barnado Photo Library, p10
Beamish, The North of England Open Air Museum, pp13 (top right), 40, 59
Bridgeman, p19
British Library, p27
Corbis, pp20, 21, 23, 48, 60 (left)
ET Archive, p50
Hulton Deutsch Collection, pp11, 42-43, 46
Humberside County Libraries, p13 (left)
The Illustrated London New Picture Library, p43
The Ironbridge Gorge Museum, p25 (left)
Leicestershire Museums (Newton Collection), p15
Mansell Collection, pp10 (bottom), 14, 24, 35, 39, 44-45
Mary Evans Picture Library, pp7, 9, 22, 23 (both), 24, 28 (both), 51, 52, 53
Bradford Metropolitan Libraries, p41
National Coal Mining Museum for England, p25 (right)
National Portrait Gallery, pp4, 35 (bottom)
National Postal Museum, p13 (bottom right)
National Railway Museum, p16
Punch, p32
Skyscan/© LAPL, p19
University Library, Keele, p31]
Wood Visual Communications, pp38-39

Editors: Saskia Gwinn and Joanne Mitchell
Layout artist: Suzanne Ward
Illustrations: Peter Dennis of Linda Rogers Associates, Tony Randell of Tony Randell
Illustration
Cover design: Blayney Partnership
Cover image: John Thomson/Getty Images

Printed and bound by L.E.G.O. S.p.A., Lavis (TN) Italy.

Contents

1 The Victorian Age

From 1837 to 1901, Great Britain had a queen called Queen Victoria. In those days Britain was very powerful, and it ruled many overseas countries including Canada and parts of Africa. These countries made up the British Empire, and Victoria was their queen too.

Britain was the world's greatest shipbuilding country; its navy helped to keep control of overseas countries and its cargo boats brought their cotton, rubber, metal and other products to Britain. British factories turned these products into finished goods. For example, the cotton was turned into cloth for making clothes. Then the goods were sold at a profit. Factory owners grew very rich but their workers were often badly paid, especially at the start of Victoria's reign.

There were many important changes during Victoria's reign. In 1837, most people lived in villages and worked on the land; by 1901 many had moved into towns to find work in factories, shops and offices. The growth of towns went on throughout Queen Victoria's reign, and so did the efforts to stop them getting too filthy and crowded.

A time of change

The two drawings below (**Source A**) show Swindon (a town in Wiltshire) at the start and end of Victoria's reign.

Which drawing is the earlier one? Why do you think so? List some of the changes which you can see. What things are the same? What do the changes tell you about people's lives during Queen Victoria's reign?

Source A

Source B *Back-to-back Victorian housing.*

In a time of change the Queen was a very important figure. She stood for things that mattered to people, for example, she made them feel proud to be British, and they admired her respectable family life. In 1887 and 1897 there were huge Jubilee (or anniversary) celebrations to mark her fiftieth and sixtieth years as Queen.

Is there a Jubilee Street near you?

Some towns have streets called Jubilee Street.

1. When do you think these streets were built?
2. See if your town has streets named after Queen Victoria, her husband Albert or the Jubilees. (A street map may help you.)
3. Try to check when the houses were built. (One of them may have a special stone which gives the date.)

Victorian children – rich and poor

Look at **Sources B** and **C**.

1. Why do you think the houses were built back-to-back?
2. How did people heat their homes?
3. Describe the activities which took place in a backyard.
4. Which children are poor and which are well off?
5. How can you tell whether the girl with the basket is poor or well-off?
6. Look at the well off children's faces. What might they be thinking?

Source C

This book is about life in Britain during Victoria's reign. This period (1837–1901) is sometimes called the Victorian Age.

② The Spread of Steam Power

For hundreds of years, villagers in Britain had farmed the land with sickles and other simple tools. As well as growing food for themselves they made their own cloth by spinning and weaving the wool from their sheep or the fibres from plants. Some earned money by spinning and weaving in their homes. They did this using simple looms which they worked by hand.

Source A *A handloom weaver's cottage.*

The power of steam was not discovered until the end of the 17th century. The first steam engines were used to pump water out of flooded mines. Then, in the 18th century, they were sometimes used in factories to work machines.

Steam-powered machines could do spinning and weaving far quicker than they could be done by hand. Soon there was no paid work for people to do in their cottages, and countryfolk had to leave their homes and find jobs in the factories.

Source B *Mule spinning.*

By the start of Queen Victoria's reign, enormous factories were being built, and towns for the workers grew up near them.

More people left the countryside as steam-powered machines replaced workers on farms. Thousands of families crowded into the towns each year to find work in the factories.

Source C

Source D

Source D shows men working on a farm. The men have a steam engine. It runs on coal and can pull heavy loads along like a tractor. (This sort of engine is sometimes called a traction engine.) This time the engine is standing still and working the other machine, which threshes corn (beats it to separate the seeds from the stalks).

Life after steam

Read these pages carefully and look at the Sources.

Discuss with a partner how the coming of steam has changed people's lives. Copy and complete the chart. Give a reason why.

Person	How life changed	Better or worse
Landowner Farmworker Factory owner Handloom weaver Children		

Sometimes there were not enough jobs for everyone, even in towns with factories. Workers were often paid very badly, but those without work got nothing at all. Some families starved but others went to live in a workhouse.

In the workhouse, people were kept alive but treated as harshly as possible. This was to make sure families would avoid going there unless they were really desperate.

Husbands, wives and children had to live apart, and no one could have any outings, visitors, tobacco or beer.

Everyone – apart from old folk and disabled people – had to do back-breaking work. For example, they had to smash rocks to pieces, ready for use in mending roads.

A workhouse yard.

Source A *Men working in the workhouse.*

In 1865, the *Daily Telegraph* described how a man had died at home because he could not face life in a workhouse:

He and his son used to work night and day repairing boots to try ... and pay for the room ... so as to keep the home together. On Friday night, when they had not even a halfpenny to buy a candle, he got up from his bench and began to shiver. He threw down the boots, saying, "Someone else must finish these when I am gone, for I can do no more." There was no fire, and he said, "I would be better if I was warm."

His wife ... took two pairs of ... boots to sell at the shop, but she could only get [enough for] coal and a little tea and bread, and her husband died on Saturday morning. When she was asked why they did not go into the workhouse the wife replied:
"We wanted the comforts of our little home."

Someone asked what the comforts were, for he only saw a little straw in the corner of the room, the windows of which were broken. The wife began to cry, and said that they had a quilt and other little things. Once, when the man applied ... for aid, the ... officer gave him a 4lb loaf and told him that if he came again he should get the 'stones'.

The son explained why they could not spend the winter in the workhouse:
"When we came out in the summer we should be like people dropped from the sky. No one would know us, and we would not have even a room. I could work now if I had food, for my sight would get better."

Life in the workhouse

Use the extract from the *Daily Telegraph*.

1. Write a list of rules people had to obey in the workhouse. Include rules you have read about but also add some rules of your own.
2. Turn your list of rules into a notice for the classroom wall.

Home sweet home?

Read the description from the *Daily Telegraph* and look at **Source A**.

1. What do you know about the family's food, heating, lighting and bedding?
2. What happened to the boots once the family had mended them?
3. What do you think the officer meant by the 'stones'? (See **Source C** also.)
4. What were the family's reasons for avoiding the workhouse?
5. Describe the workers' seats. Why do you think they were made like this?

Thomas Barnardo provided hostels where hundreds of homeless children could live.

Some Victorians tried to help people who were being ill-treated. At the start of Queen Victoria's reign, Elizabeth Fry called for better conditions in prisons, especially for women.

Better conditions

Look at **Source B** which shows Elizabeth Fry visiting a prison.

1. Try to pick out Elizabeth Fry in the painting.
   What do you think she is doing?
2. Fry has brought some visitors to the prison. Which are the visitors and which are the prisoners? How can you tell?
3. What happened to children if their mothers were sent to prison?
4. Does this prison seem as bad as the one Dickens describes? In what way does it seem different?
5. Fry always tried to see every part of the prisons she visited. Why do you think this was so important?

Source B

Source C *Breaking stones.*

Writers like Dickens made sure no one forgot the cruel way many workers and prisoners were treated.

For example, in *The Pickwick Papers* he described a prison where people went if they were in debt:

Mr Tom Roker ... led the way through an iron gate.   •
"Oh," said Mr Pickwick, looking down a dark and filthy staircase, which appeared to lead to a row of damp and gloomy stone caverns beneath the ground ... "You don't really mean to say that human beings live down in those wretched dungeons."
"Live down there! Yes, and die down there, too, very often," replied Mr Roker; "and what of that?"

Until Queen Victoria's time, most people spent their lives in the village where they were born. They might go to market in a neighbouring town but they rarely went further.

Some business people did make long journeys. Often they travelled in the horse-drawn stage coaches that linked London with other parts of the country.

Shorter journeys were usually made on foot or on horseback. Horses were very important indeed for transporting goods. They pulled farm wagons along country roads and they hauled heavy barges along canals. They also hauled wagons of coal, stone and other supplies. Often the wagons were linked together to form long trains, and the horses pulled them along special tracks. Sometimes goods were taken from barges and put into wagons to finish their journey.

The horse-drawn 'trains' developed into proper railways. Steam engines fixed at the top of a hill were sometimes used to haul wagons up by means of chains. Then people started to fix an engine at the front of a train. The engine travelled along a track and pulled the train with it.

Source A

Stage coaches and trains

Read this page carefully and look at **Source A**.

1. **Source A** was painted in Queen Victoria's reign. What was the artist saying about the two forms of transport?
2. How did the invention of the railway change people's lives?
3. Did some people benefit more than others?

Source B *Lady Mary.*

Source C *Locomotive at Beamish Museum.*

Industrial locomotives

Look at **Source B**.

1. One man drove the engine and the other stoked the boiler. Describe what job each man is doing.
2. Compare **Sources B** and **C**. Is the Beamish train a good reconstruction? Give reasons for your answer.
3. Why do you think museums reconstruct trains?
4. Make a list of people who might want to see and ride old locomotives. Can you think of different reasons they might have?
5. Draw an old locomotive. Find out about it and label the parts.

New railway tracks were quickly built. One of the most important linked Stockton and Darlington in the north of England. It was opened in 1825 and some people say it was the first proper railway in the world. Not only did the trains have locomotives (engines on wheels) but anyone could use them for goods or travel (other railways were private).

Railways were soon being built throughout Britain. By the middle of Queen Victoria's reign, nearly every big town and village had a station.

A special year

Look at **Source D**.

1. The stamp appeared in 1975, 150 years after something special had happened. What was it?
2. Why was the event special?
3. How do you know this stamp was not produced in 1825?

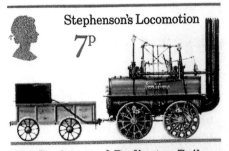

Stephenson's Locomotion
7ᵖ
1825 Stockton and Darlington Railway
Source D

13

5 Navvies at Work

Railway builders had a very hard and dangerous life. The men (called navvies) worked with spades and barrows to take away unwanted soil. Often, the men lived in camps beside new railway lines.

Source A

NAVVY IN HEAVY MARCHING ORDER.

A writer described the conditions at the time:

Some slept in huts constructed of damp turf, cut from the wet grass, too low to stand upright in ... Others formed a room of stones ... The rain beat through the roof, and ... the wind swept through the holes. If they caught a fever they died, or wandered in the open air, spreading the disease wherever they went. In these huts they lived with their women.

In 1846, a railway boss described to some members of Parliament how he treated his workers.

The men live in wooden buildings, with a room for cooking and ... hammocks slung along each side.
"One man's wife cooks for the whole of them?"
"Yes."
"You do not allow any other women in the camp?"
"No."

The navvy

Look at **Source A** and read the description of life on the railway.

1. List the things the navvy is carrying. In each case, suggest why he needed it.
2. Look at the two descriptions of the navvies' camps. Which camp seems to be better? Why?
3. Who is asking the questions in the second paragraph?
4. Do you think the navvies would have liked a chance to give their opinions too? Why?
5. Why might a navvy be afraid to complain?

Some railway workers had come from Ireland to escape from starvation. Many Irish people lived on potatoes, which they grew on their own small plots of land. In the late 1840s, the potato plants were hit by disease and the crops were poor.

Some Irish people found jobs and homes in English cities. Others helped to build railways. Because they were used to a very hard life they often did the hardest, most dangerous jobs, like digging tunnels and using explosives.

A navvies' camp.

Think about the life of a navvy.

1. Suggest some of the dangers they faced in their work.
2. How might working conditions have been improved?
3. Why do you think such improvements were not made?

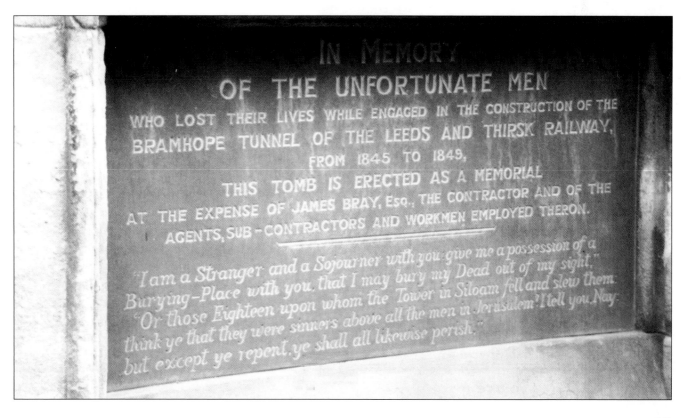

IN MEMORY
OF THE UNFORTUNATE MEN
WHO LOST THEIR LIVES WHILE ENGAGED IN THE CONSTRUCTION OF THE
BRAMHOPE TUNNEL OF THE LEEDS AND THIRSK RAILWAY,
FROM 1845 TO 1849,
THIS TOMB IS ERECTED AS A MEMORIAL
AT THE EXPENSE OF JAMES BRAY, ESQ., THE CONTRACTOR AND OF THE
AGENTS, SUB-CONTRACTORS AND WORKMEN EMPLOYED THEREON.

"I am a Stranger and a Sojourner with you give me a possession of a Burying-Place with you, that I may bury my Dead out of my sight." "Or those Eighteen upon whom the Tower in Siloam fell and slew them, think ye that they were sinners above all the men in Jerusalem? I tell you Nay: but except ye repent, ye shall all likewise perish."

Trains were much quicker than coaches. A train could travel from Scotland to London in one day or night; people going by coach had to sleep in different inns on the way. Shorter journeys might take half an hour by train instead of half a day by coach.

Travel became much cheaper and easier; a coach had room for 10 or 12 people, a train could take hundreds.

Source B *First class travel.*

Source A

People had different views about the trains. One man had this to say:

Everything is near, everything is immediate – time, distance and delay are removed.

Some people did not like the railways. This is what someone else had to say:

I detest railways. Your railway has cut through and spoiled some of the loveliest bits of scenery in the country.

Now, every fool in Buxton can be in Bakewell in half an hour, and every fool in Bakewell can be at Buxton.

Source C *Second class travel.*

Source D *Third class travel.*

First class travel?

Look at **Sources B**, **C** and **D**.

1. Describe the differences between the carriages.
2. At the start of Queen Victoria's reign, someone wrote, 'Get as far from the engine as possible'. Try to think of some reasons for this.
3. Which sort of carriage do you think was nearest the engine? Which do you think was furthest from it? Say why you think so.

The poorest workers were forced to stay in their smoky cities. Better off people could live in smaller towns and travel to work; they could also go away for holidays.

Rail travel

Read page 16.

1. What effect did the train have on the journey time between Scotland and London?
2. Look again at what the people said about railways. What did they like and dislike about them?
3. Say what you feel about the points they made.
4. How do you and your friends think trains affected the following:
   - factory owners
   - stage coach and canal companies and their employees
   - towns like Swindon (look again at **Source A** on pages 4 and 5)
   - seaside towns like Blackpool
   - the range of fresh food which people ate
   - the spread of news and ideas
   - the very poor.

Scotland to London

According to a Victorian writer, 'The early Scotsman scratches himself in the morning mists of the north, and has his porridge in London before the setting sun'.

1. Discuss what the writer meant.
2. Describe what the poster (**Source A**) is advertising.
3. How might people who saw the poster respond?

The list below shows how Swindon grew during Queen Victoria's reign.

Mark each new area on the map (**Source E**), using a different colour for each. Label the map clearly.
- The railway from London to Bristol, including Swindon station.
- The railway from Swindon to Gloucester.
- The locomotive works just west of the place where the railways joined.
- The small area of rail workers' houses south of the junction.
- The carriage and wagon works north of the junction.
- The large triangular area of houses and shops between the London–Bristol railway and Old Swindon.
- The railway from Andover to Cheltenham.
- Other new housing areas near the railway works.

During Queen Victoria's reign, railways were built linking Swindon to other towns and cities. Travel and communication became easier and the village grew into a large town.

Aerial picture of Swindon in the early 2000s.

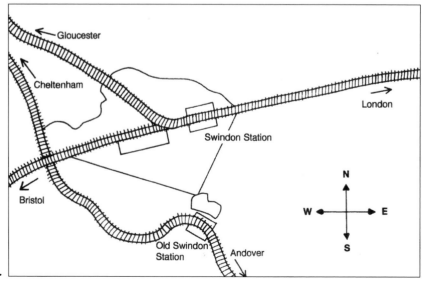

Source E *Map of Swindon.*

Full Speed Ahead!

Source F shows how many hours it took to get from London to other major cities at different dates.

Source G compares how far people could travel, in one hour, in different years during Queen Victoria's reign.

How far people could travel in an hour.

	1837	1850	1900
The rich	8 miles by coach	30 miles by rail	42 miles by rail
The poor	4 miles on foot	4 miles on foot	

Source G

Source F

From London to		Birmingham	Brighton	Exeter	Halifax	Liverpool	Norwich
1837	**Road**	11	6	18	23	24	13.5
1850	**Rail**	3	1.5	5	7	6.5	6
1900	**Rail**	2.5	1.5	4	4.5	4	4

Then and now

Study **Sources F** and **G**.

1. Coaches travelled further each day in summer than they did in winter. Suggest two reasons for this.
2. Do you think journeys are much faster today than they were in 1900? What helps people to travel faster today? What slows them down?

Large numbers of people moved to the towns to find work in the mills. Many mill workers lived in cramped and filthy conditions. The rows of houses were built 'back-to-back', and this meant that each house had other houses attached on three sides. Only the front of each house could have windows, and these looked out on a narrow road or alleyway.

There was usually one room upstairs and one room downstairs. A family of up to 10 or 12 people might have to share this tiny home, and sometimes three or four of them had to share one bed.

Mrs Gaskell, a Victorian writer, described a visit to such a home:

You went down into the cellar in which a family of human beings lived. It was very dark inside ... the smell was so fetid [foul] as almost to knock the two men down ... You could just see three or four little children rolling on the wet brick floor, through which the moisture of the street oozed up; the fireplace was empty and black; the wife sat on her husband's lair [bed] and cried in the dark loneliness.

Source A

Back alleys

Look at **Source A**.

1. When do you think this was taken?
2. Make a list of activities people might have done in 'back alleys'.
3. Describe what it would have been like at night.

Life in a cellar

The drawing on the right (**Source C**), done in Victorian times, shows a cellar home. Like Mrs Gaskell, the artist is trying to tell us about the lives of the poor. Use the drawing and Mrs Gaskell's description to help you answer the following questions:

1. What is the worst thing about the cellar described by Mrs Gaskell? What do you think has caused this problem?
2. Why do you think the fireplace is empty?
3. A lair is a place where an animal hides. Why do you think Mrs Gaskell chose that particular word?
4. Look at the people in the drawing and study their faces. What do you think their feelings are?
5. What are the woman and oldest child doing?
6. Do you think the woman has warm or cold water? If it is warm, how did she heat it? Where do you think she got the water?

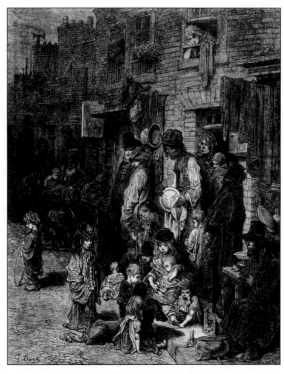

Source B

Street life

Look at **Source B** of the street scene.

1. What do you think the men are doing?
2. What are the people selling?
3. What does this picture tell you about family life in Victorian times?
4. Do you think the family in the centre was poor or better off? Give a reason for your answer.

Source C

Source A

Source B

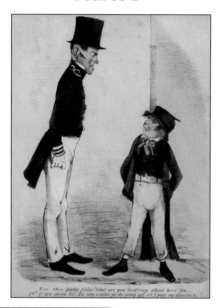

Victorian police

Sources A and **B** show policemen in Queen Victoria's reign.

1. Which one do you think is the earlier one? Why?
2. Look at **Source A**. Write a story, play or strip cartoon for which the picture is an illustration. Remember what things were like in Victorian times.

Slang words

The Victorians used all sorts of slang words when they talked about crime and criminals.

Draw lines to link the slang name with the correct description.

Drag Sneaks	people who cut the panes out of shop windows.
Star Glazers	people who steal goods or luggage from carts or coaches.
Dead Lurkers	people who empty tills when the shopkeeper's back is turned.
Till-friskers	people who steal coats and umbrellas at dusk or on Sunday afternoons.
Mudlarks	people who steal pieces of rope and lumps of coal from ships tied up at the riverside.
Noisy Racket Men	people who steal china or glass from outside china shops.

This passage describes the crimes and punishments of a young criminal, Thomas Miller.

Thomas Miller, aged 8 years, was tried at Clerkenwell in August, 1845, for stealing boxes. The judge sentenced him to be imprisoned for one month and whipped.

In January, 1846, he was again tried for robbing a till. He was sentenced to 7 years transportation, but his sentence was cut to three months in prison.

Source C *A prisoner is held at Newgate Prison during Victorian times.*

Prison life

Look at **Source C**.

Pretend you are Mrs Fry. Write a report about the conditions in which Thomas is being kept.

The criminal Thomas Miller

Different conversations took place between the judge, Thomas, Mrs Fry (the prison reformer), and the man who was robbed. The conversations happened at different times.

Fill in the speech bubbles with what you think each person might have said.

1845

Judge: What is your excuse?
Thomas:

Judge: Too harsh? Why?
Mrs Fry:

1846

Judge: What is your excuse this time?
Thomas:

Thomas: What's transportation?
Mrs Fry:

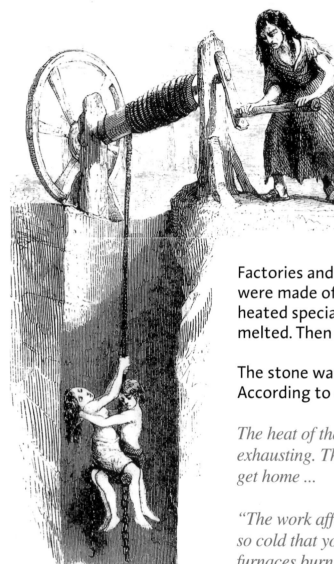

Source A

Factories and railways needed machines and engines which were made of metal. To get metal, Victorian workers heated special stone (called ore) until the metal inside it melted. Then they let the metal run into moulds to harden.

The stone was heated in giant ovens called furnaces. According to one Victorian writer:

The heat of the furnaces is terrible and the work most exhausting. The men have to wring their clothes when they get home ...

"The work affects you all over," said a worker ... "You get so cold that you shiver so you can't hold your food. The furnaces burn the insides out of you."

The man had burns all over his body.

A working life

Read carefully the descriptions of Victorian workers on these pages.

1. Why do you think the metal workers had to wring their clothes out when they got home?
2. One particular furnace worker is mentioned. What is wrong with him?
3. What word is used for a coal miner?
4. How can you tell that the cavern where the miner is working is small?
5. Describe what the children in **Source A** are doing.

Working in coal mines was just as unpleasant. Workers had to go down shafts (deep holes in the ground) to get to the coal. They climbed down ladders or were lowered on ropes, and there was always the chance of a terrible fall. At the bottom, the dangers were even worse. To get to the coal, they had to go along narrow tunnels. Sometimes there was so little room that they had to crawl on their hands and knees or slide on their stomachs. In the darkness they could hear water trickling down through the rocks.

This is how a Victorian writer described the scene which a worker would find at the end of his tunnel:

*In a cavern full of floating coal dust ...
glimmer three or four candles stuck in clay.
One hewer, nearly naked, lying upon his
back, has his small, sharp pick-axe a little
above his nose and picking into the coal ...*

Iron works, Coalbrookdale.

A life of danger

Using candles in a mine was especially dangerous.

1. Try to find out the reasons for this.
2. What other dangers faced Victorian miners? You can probably think of three or four by yourself (or with your friends).
3. What effects did the building of iron works have on the environment?

Ancient or modern?

Look at the small photograph below (**Source B**). It was taken in a modern museum and shows what conditions were like for children who worked in the mines.

1. How well do the conditions match those shown in **Source A**?
2. Do you think the museum used modern books or Victorian books for its information?
3. Which would be better? Why do you think so?
4. What other sources of information might the museum have used?

Source B

At the start of Queen Victoria's reign, women and children had to work for long hours, even if their jobs were very tiring indeed. In mines, the women and children had to take the coal to the wagons at the surface. **Sources A** and **B** are drawings (found in Victorian books) of children moving through a tunnel and women and children working in mills.

This is what starting work was like for a seven-year-old called Robert Blincoe:

They reached the mill at about half past five ... Blincoe smelt the fumes of the oil on the axles of 20 000 wheels and spindles.

The task first given to him was to pick up the loose cotton that fell onto the floor ... Nothing could be easier, although he was terrified by the whirling motion and noise of the machinery, and not a little affected by the dust ... Unused to the stench, he soon felt sick, and by constantly stooping, his back ached ... But he soon found that sitting down was strictly forbidden. His task-master said he must keep on his legs. He did so for six hours and a half, suffering greatly with hunger and thirst.

Blincoe had grown up by the start of Victoria's reign, but children were still being treated in the same harsh way.

Source B

Source A

Source C

Victorian children

Look at the girls in **Source C**.

1. What jobs do you think they do?
2. What is your evidence?

A working life

Bosses were often harsh and cruel but they allowed their workers to have a lunch break.

1. Why do you think they gave them a break?
2. Mining families often worked together. Do you think they were paid by the hour or by how much coal they produced in a day? Why do you think so?
3. Compare Robert's description of life in the mill with **Sources B** and **D**. How are they the same and how are they different?

Women and children

Read these pages and look carefully at the sources.

1. How was the moving of coal dangerous?
2. List some of the things which made Robert Blincoe's morning unpleasant.
3. Why do you think some workers only saw daylight on Sundays?

People believed that Sunday was a day for resting and attending church, so nearly everyone had this day off work each week.

Many churches ran Sunday schools, and this was the only schooling many children got. However, some were so tired that they fell asleep and fell off their benches during the lessons.

Working in mills could be almost as hard as working in mines. It was dangerous too, for workers sometimes got caught in machines, and growing children were crippled by all the bending and standing they had to do.

Source D

Come All You Cotton Weavers

Words and music adapted from *100 Songs of Toil* ed. K. Dallas.

Come all you cot-ton wea-vers your looms you must pull down. You must
get new jobs in fac-tor-ies in coun-try or in town, For
our cot-ton mas-ters have found out a cle-ver scheme; These
cot-ton goods now wove by hand they're going to weave by steam.

If you go up my stair-way there's three or four fine looms, And
they are stand-ing emp-ty just fill-ing up the room, And
if you ask the rea-son why, the mo-ther tells you plain, Her
daugh-ters have for-sa-ken them and gone to weave by steam.

So hur-ry all you wea-vers for you must rise up soon, And
you must work in fac-tor-ies and go home by the moon. You
can-not tend your gar-dens for you must live in town, And
you must make your shut-tle fly and mind your mas-ter's frown.

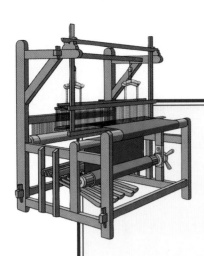

Come All You Cotton Weavers

Verse 1

Come all you cotton weavers
your looms you must pull down.
You must get new jobs in factories
in country or in town,
For our cotton masters have
found out a clever scheme;
These cotton goods now wove by hand
they're going to weave by steam.

Verse 2

If you go up my stairway
there's three or four fine looms,
And they are standing empty
just filling up the room,
And if you ask the reason why,
the mother tells you plain,
Her daughters have forsaken them
and gone to weave by steam.

Verse 3

So hurry all you weavers
for you must rise up soon,
And you must work in factories
and go home by the moon.
You cannot tend your gardens
for you must live in town,
And you must make your shuttle fly
and mind your master's frown.

For most of Queen Victoria's reign, chimney sweeps employed young children to go up chimneys and sweep them clean. The work was very dangerous, for the soot got into children's lungs and into cuts on their arms and legs.

An adult chimney sweep explained what life was like for a young chimney sweep:

The flesh must be hardened. This is done by rubbing it, chiefly on the elbows and knees, with the strongest brine. You must stand over them with a cane or coax them by a promise of a halfpenny if they will stand a few more rubs. At first they will come back from their work with their arms and knees streaming with blood and the knees looking as if the caps had been pulled off. Then they must be rubbed with brine again and perhaps go off to another chimney.

The best age for teaching boys is about six. But I have known at least two of my neighbours' children begin at the age of five.

Seven or eight years ago a boy was smothered (suffocated) in a chimney here. The doctor who opened his body said that they had pulled his heart and liver all over the place in dragging him down.

Source A

A law had been passed in 1840 to put a stop to the use of children, but people who broke the law were only fined a small sum, and most sweeps carried on as before. Their crimes were made public.

Societies were formed to make sure that people obeyed the law. Some of these Societies offered to sweep people's chimneys without using boys, and they produced cards and leaflets to let people know about their work. The card below was produced in part of Staffordshire called the Pottery or Potteries.

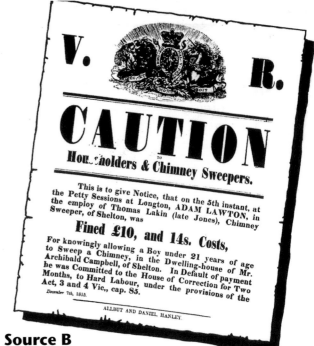

Source B
Public notice.

Advertising new methods.

The law

Look at the public notice (**Source B**).

1. Why was Adam Lawton fined?
2. How much was he fined?
3. Did he pay the fine?
4. How was he punished?
5. Who do you think produced the notice? Why was it produced?

Chimney sweeps

You will need to read these pages carefully.

1. Find out what brine is. What did chimney sweeps use it for?
2. How can you tell that the brine must have hurt?
3. What were the dangers children faced when they went up chimneys?
4. What could sweeps use instead of children?
5. Why do you think people risked a fine rather than changing their methods?

Climbing boys

Look at the boy in **Source A**.

1. How old do you think he is?
2. What is he holding?
3. Where is he standing?
4. What job has he done?
5. Why were small children used to sweep chimneys?

Source A

THE "SILENT HIGHWAY"-MAN.

Some people cared very deeply about how workers were treated. One of these people was Lord Ashley, who later became the Earl of Shaftesbury.

Shaftesbury and others called for changes to stop children being worn out and crippled by their work. In 1833 (four years before the start of Queen Victoria's reign), Parliament passed a Factory Bill. It banned the use of children under nine in mills and it put a limit on older children's working hours. However, the hours were still very long, and adults were not protected at all. In any case, some employers simply ignored the new laws.

In 1842, Parliament banned the use of women, girls and young boys in coal mines. Then, in 1844 and 1847, it cut the number of hours that women and children could work in mills. Children from nine to thirteen could work for up to six and a half hours a day, and women and older children could work for up to ten hours a day.

Parliament placed a limit on the workers' hours. It tried to see that younger children had some part-time schooling, and schools were often set up at factories. Finally, in 1875, Parliament made a tough new law that stopped the use of climbing boys. Inspectors checked that bosses were obeying all the new laws.

At the start of Queen Victoria's reign, very few homes had their own water supply. Many homes did not have toilets, and slops were poured into the gutters. Other homes had toilets outside which did not flush and the filth went into a hole in the ground. It even got into the water used for drinking and washing, which came out of wells and public taps. Sometimes the water looked and smelled dirty; but even when it seemed to be clean it was full of germs; and deadly diseases, such as typhoid, spread through many cities. In the centre of Manchester, most people died before they were twenty.

Early in Queen Victoria's reign, a man called Edwin Chadwick said that every home should have its own toilet linked to a sewer. He also said that every home should have clean running water. By 1901, flush toilets, sewers and running water were provided in many homes. As a result, there was far less disease.

Health conditions

Read these pages carefully and look at **Sources A** and **B**.

1. Look at **Source B**. In which areas were the homes most overcrowded?
2. Which classes of people lived in the unhealthiest places? Explain your answer.
3. The cartoon in **Source A** was drawn in Queen Victoria's reign. What do you think the artist was trying to say?

Key

⬛	Houses of the working classes
⬛	Shops, warehouses and houses of tradespeople
⬜	Houses of the upper class

Ward	Population	Population of each acre
Nos I & II	28 775	207
III, IV & V	23 039	118
VI, VII & VIII	30 306	84

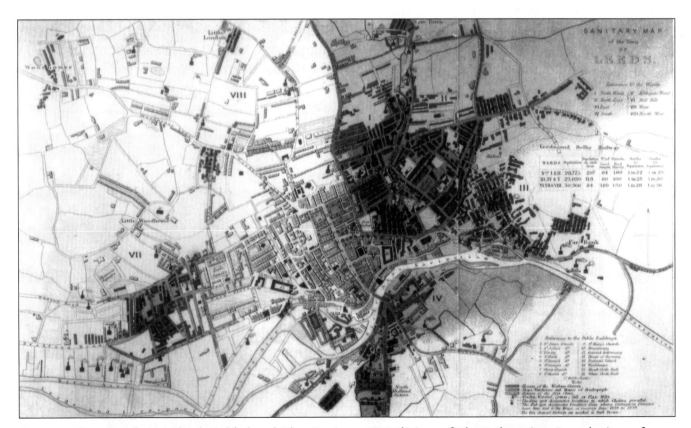

Source B *Map from Chadwick's book* The Sanitary Condition of The Labouring Population of Great Britain.

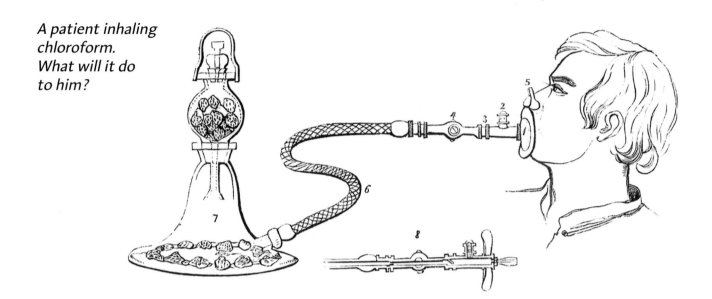

A patient inhaling chloroform. What will it do to him?

Medical treatment also improved during Victorian times. At the start of Queen Victoria's reign, it was hard to carry out operations because doctors had no reliable way of easing pain, and a team of men had to hold the screaming patient down. Surgeons had to be very quick, and could only do simple operations like cutting off legs. They could not do any delicate work inside patients' bodies. During the 1840s, the problem was solved by the use of anaesthetics (drugs, such as ether and chloroform, which deadened pain).

Surgeons using chloroform could do all sorts of new operations, but some patients died because germs got into their wounds. Doctors were only beginning to understand about germs, but a Scottish surgeon called Joseph Lister began to use an antiseptic (or germ-killing) spray during operations. Later, he and other surgeons simply kept themselves, their tools and their hospitals as clean and germ-free as possible.

Thanks to Chadwick's ideas, Victorian people began to live longer and healthier lives. And if they did fall ill they could often be treated and cured.

Using an antiseptic spray for an operation.

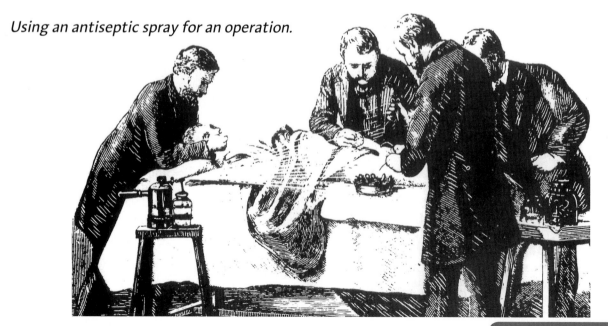

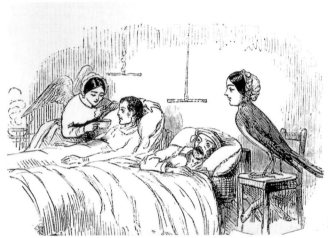

An English nurse called Florence Nightingale went to the Crimea (southern Russia) to tend soldiers wounded in battle there. She helped to spread the idea that nurses and hospitals should be clean.

Source C

Source D *Florence Nightingale, at Scutari.*

Some Victorians felt it was wrong to use anaesthetics, especially for easing the pain of childbirth. They pointed out a Bible verse that seemed to say that giving birth was meant to be painful. However, in 1857 Queen Victoria used chloroform herself.

Improvements in medicine

1. The painting in **Source C** includes two pictures of Florence Nightingale's face. What was the artist trying to say about her?
2. Describe what has happened in the painting in **Source D**.
3. What effect do you think Queen Victoria's action had on other people?
4. What message was the artist trying to convey?

What the papers say

At the end of Queen Victoria's reign, there was a quarrel between British settlers in southern Africa and Dutch settlers, known as Boers. Under their President, Paul Kruger, the Boers ruled an area known as the Transvaal, but Britain wanted to take it over. In October 1899, the Boers sent Britain an ultimatum (a solemn warning) threatening war.

We all think about things in different ways.

"Oh dear! It's half empty!"

"Ah good! It's half full!"

Writers are the same as everyone else.
Their opinions and attitudes show up clearly in what they say about an event. You can see this if you compare reports in different newspapers.

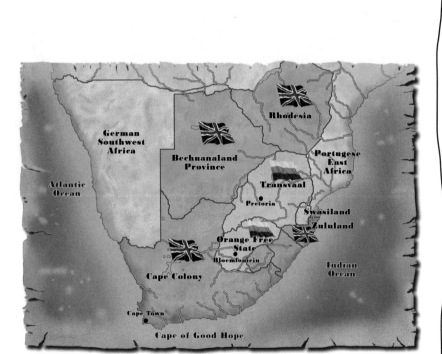

The key areas of the Boer War.

WAR!

The bolt has fallen. The Transvaal Government has sent to Great Britain an ultimatum which means war. Some of our public writers can only cry out 'Insolent!' 'Impudent!' and call upon the ... Government to teach these rude people a lesson. But ... the Transvaal Government waited as long as there was the slightest hope of peace.

We would have preferred to see our soldiers fighting in a necessary and more glorious cause.

Bradford Telegraph

'An Insult to Britain'

Hope is no longer possible ... A challenge ... is flung down to us by a little country. The Boers ... were determined to decide their argument with us by the sword, and by the sword it must now be decided.

The Times

'Kruger's War'

What is President Kruger going to war about? ... It is said that the Boers are fighting for their independence and that the aim of Great Britain has been to force them into war. How can these statements be true? President Kruger has declared war because he preferred to do so.

Daily News

Like Rats in a Trap

The Government of the Transvaal has presented an ultimatum to the British Government ... We cannot ... be greatly surprised at it. That the Boers, seeing themselves caught like rats in a trap, did not some days ago strike a despairing blow... is one more proof... that they want peace.

Morning Leader

Headline news

Look at the different newspaper reports in this chapter.

Discuss how the newspapers differ and then complete the following sentences with the word **peace** or **war**.

- According to the *Bradford Telegraph*, the Boers want _____ .
- According to *The Times*, the Boers want _____ .
- According to the *Daily News*, the Boerswant _____.
- According to the *Morning Leader*, the Boers want _____.

A news story

Choose a method of investigating how news reports differ.

1. Collect different newspapers and read what they say about a recent event. How do they differ?

   OR

2. Agree with friends to write separate reports about something which has happened in your town or classroom. Discuss the differences. Why do writers differ so much in what they say?

14 Saltaire Village

There were many mill owners who treated their workers cruelly, but others tried to meet their needs and give them homes that were fit to live in.

One man who treated his workers well was Sir Titus Salt. In the 1850s he built his own spinning and weaving mills, along with a village to house the workers.

Salt made sure that everything was clean and healthy. He chose a site in the Yorkshire countryside, well away from the smoke and filth of the nearest cities (Leeds and Bradford). Because the village was totally new, it needed a name, and Salt decided to call it Saltaire (made up from his own name and that of the nearby River Aire).

There were no oozing gutters outside the doors, for every house had a toilet linked to underground drains.

There was water on tap, and every home had gas lamps, at least in the downstairs rooms. There were lots of large windows to let in plenty of daylight and air, and some houses even had their own gardens. Workers rented the houses for 1 shilling (5p) a week!

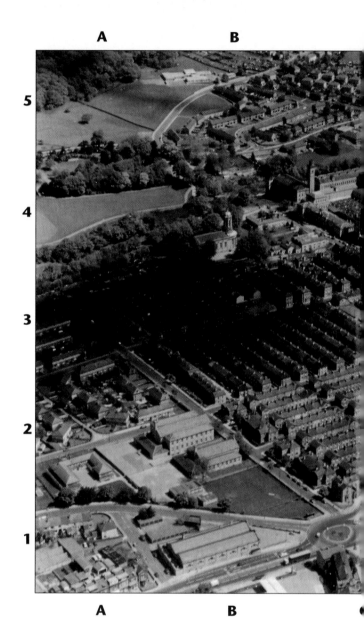

Most of the houses in Salt's village had two rooms downstairs and two rooms upstairs. The rooms were small but at least there was no need for parents and children to share a bed.

The village included a church, a park and a library for the workers to use.

Source A *Saltaire from the air.*

D   E

5

4

3

2

1

D   E

Saltaire

Look at the photograph of Saltaire from the air (**Source A**). It will help you to answer the following questions.

1. Was the photograph taken in Salt's time or ours? How do you know?
2. Do you think all the houses shown in the photograph were built by Salt?
3. Try to pick out some of the housing built in Salt's time. Use the grid to help you.
4. Can you find Salt's mill?

Now look at **Source B**. It shows Saltaire shortly after it was built.

5. Suggest some of the ways in which goods and people travelled to and from the village.
6. The village had no public house. Why do you think this was?
7. At the end of some blocks of houses there were larger houses. Suggest which workers might have lived there.
8. One house had a tower where someone could keep an eye on the villagers. How do you think they felt about being watched in this way?

Source B

Hymns such as *All Things Bright and Beautiful* encouraged the poor to accept their hard lives while rich folk lived in luxury. Salt's workers had homes with only two rooms, but a nearby mansion called Milner Field had over 50 rooms. There was a billiard room, a library and a music room with a huge organ. There was also a giant conservatory with marble statues and tropical plants. Every room was as comfortable and fine as possible, with beautiful carpets and chandeliers. The mansion was owned by Titus Salt (Sir Titus Salt's son).

Salt had a horse-drawn coach to take him wherever he wanted. To reach the mill he travelled down a tree-lined drive and across his own bridge. Salt and his family had over a dozen maids and servants. They treated them well but they had to work hard.

Many Victorian girls became maids, though few worked in mansions like Milner Field. Some worked in farmhouses; others found jobs in the homes of well-paid workers like bank managers. They had to sleep in the cellar or attic, and often they shared it with other maids and perhaps a number of mice or rats.

Maids were paid just a few pence a week but they got enough food to keep them alive. It was usually better to become a maid than to stay at home in a filthy slum.

Maids had to do all sorts of housework, and in those days it was harder than it is today. For example, there were no washing machines, and maids scrubbed clothes on a scrubbing board or put them in a tub and beat them with a stick called a 'dolly'.

Often, there was a housekeeper telling the maids what to do – and boxing their ears if they did it wrong.

Source A

Source B

Victorian servants

Look at **Source A**.

1. Try to find out what each of the items was called.
2. Why do you think the 'dollies' have slots at the bottom?
3. Think about Salt's life and his home and list some of the things his maids and servants might have had to do.
4. What other servants might Titus Salt have employed to work at Milner Field mansion?

Rich and poor

The conditions in which people lived varied enormously.

Look at **Source B**. What is the artist trying to say about how rich and poor people lived?

Milner Field mansion

16 Schools

At the start of Queen Victoria's reign, few children went to school, and they grew up unable to read or write. Church registers (records) of marriages show that only half of the people who married could sign their names.

The government did not run any schools. Some people ran small schools in their homes. Larger schools, called charity schools, were built and run by wealthy people who wanted children to learn about God and Jesus Christ.

Most charity schools had a single class and just one teacher, who taught the pupils how to read the Bible and Prayer Book. She also taught them writing, arithmetic, and perhaps some skills like sewing and gardening.

Charity schools for the very poor were called 'ragged schools'. One man explained:

When we first opened the school no less than five boys came absolutely naked except for their mothers' shawls which were pinned around them. Five separate gangs of thieves attended the school.

Schools often charged a few pence a week, and many parents could not afford it; others needed the money their children could earn at work. Because of this, most children left before they were ten. The man who founded the 'ragged school' said that the thieves were 'all, within six months, earning their [livings] more or less respectably'. For some children, work and school went together. Children in textile (cloth) mills often worked in the morning and studied in the afternoon. Some bosses even provided a schoolroom at the mill.

Source A

Source B *Girls and boys were often taught separately.*

In 1843, Charles Dickens said the following about a 'ragged school' at Field Lane in London:

It was held in a low-roofed den in a sickening atmosphere in the midst of ... dirt and disease ... The pupils ... sang, fought, danced, robbed each other – seemed possessed by legions of devils.

A few years later he said it was:

Quiet and orderly ... well white-washed, numerously attended, and thoroughly well established.

Other schools were run by churches. As well as providing Sunday schools they began to open more and more day schools. Often, there was a teacher and over 100 pupils in one large room. It was hard to keep order; bad behaviour was punished severely, and many children were caned until they bled. Older pupils, called monitors, did a lot of the teaching. They stayed behind after school for extra lessons. Then, the next day, they taught small groups of younger pupils.

Some schools were very poor indeed. A government inspector said that at one school:

The children were playing in the open yard, and the master was ... sawing up the blackboard. His books and materials for teaching ... consisted of six Bibles, some copy books, one slate, half a dozen loose and ragged leaves of Reading Made Easy *and the remains of the blackboard ... supported on either side by a hand-saw and a hammer.*

Queen Victoria's government wanted every child to go to school, and they also wanted to make schools better and less overcrowded. In 1870 they told local councils to set up their own schools if extra places were needed. Then, in 1876, a new law said that children must go to school until they were twelve or thirteen.

'Ragged schools'

Think about what you have read about schools.

1. How do you think 'ragged schools' got their name? Do you think children had to pay to attend them? Why?
2. The man who founded the 'ragged school' did not mention teaching the children to read or teaching them about the Bible. What did he seem to care about most?
3. Why do you think the teacher was sawing up his blackboard? Find out why teachers and pupils used slates in Victorian schools.
4. In 1842, a teenage boy said:
   "I cannot read much ... I have read the spelling book and Ready-ma-deasy. I cannot write."
   What do you think he meant by Ready-ma-deasy? (Read this page again if you need a clue.) What does his mistake tell us?
5. Look at **Sources A** and **B**. How were Victorian classrooms different from yours?

In Victorian times, the teacher in charge of each school had to keep a 'log' (a sort of diary listing the main events).

1882 May 26

Another case of the same sort as last week happened again last Monday – a woman using insulting language in the presence of all the children. The affair arose from her boy's being sent home for his schoolmoney. The case was reported to the Clerk, & on Wed. night the Board decided to take such measures as would put a stop to all such conduct. The woman has been threatened with Law if the like occurs again. Broke up to-day for Whitsuntide.

Source C

School logs

Study the page from the school log (**Source C**).

1. What made the mother angry?
2. What do you think 'schoolmoney' was?
3. How does the children's schooling seem to differ from yours? (You can discuss this and then make a list of points.)
4. Imagine you are a pupil at Eldwick School in the 1880s and write a 'log' or diary from your own point of view. You can write about some of the days in the real log. For example, what was it like for you when the angry mother arrived?

17 Public Buildings

The Victorians were proud of their towns and cities, and they showed their pride by building magnificent town halls and libraries, many of which are still in use. They were also proud of their success in business, and we still use some of the market halls and corn and cloth exchanges they built.

Near to their towns the Victorians built sewage and water works so that people could have clean streets and clean water. At Papplewick near Nottingham the water works had steam-driven pumps to send the water to people's homes. The pumps can still be seen inside the very fine Victorian building. The Victorians showed how important they thought clean water was by decorating the inside with all sorts of water and wildlife designs.

Source A *Papplewick Pumping Station near Mansfield.*

How are they different?

The sources in this chapter show Victorian buildings.

How are they different from modern buildings?

Source B *Liverpool Street Station.*

Companies sometimes wanted people to lend them money, perhaps to buy new stock or new ships. They knew that people would only do this if the company seemed to be doing well, so they showed their wealth by spending as much as they could on their buildings. Railway companies were especially keen to attract new investors, and some of their stations look like palaces!

The Victorians built real palaces too. One of these is the Palace of Westminster, also called the Houses of Parliament. This has lots of towers and spikes, but the Victorians found out how to use metal to make archways and domes. Victorian stations have large arches, and the Albert Hall in London has an enormous dome.

Victorian buildings

Think about the buildings in a town near you.

1. Try to decide if any large buildings in your area look Victorian, then check their dates.
2. Make a list of some large Victorian buildings you know about, including ones you have seen in this book and ones in your area. You can add a note to say what the building tells you about the Victorians. Your own ideas are best but here are two examples:
   - Saltaire Church – workers were expected to go to church every Sunday
   - St Pancras Station – more and more railways were being built.

Source C *Houses of Parliament.*

Public buildings

Look carefully at this chapter.

1. What do you think was done in corn and cloth exchanges?
2. Nowadays, we rarely think about water and sewage works. Why did the Victorians care about them so much?
3. Why were the Victorians able to build huge archways and domes? Where can we see huge archways which the Victorians built?

When it is finished, the graph will show how the population of the London area grew during Queen Victoria's reign.

Each shaded figure stands for one million people.

The column for 1841 shows that just over two million people lived in the London area at that time.

 = one million people

Using the following information, copy and complete the graph.

1. In 1861 the area had three million people. In the column marked 1861, shade the bottom three figures.
2. In 1881 there were five million people. In the column marked 1881, shade the bottom five figures.
3. In 1901 there were six and a half million people. This time you decide what to do!

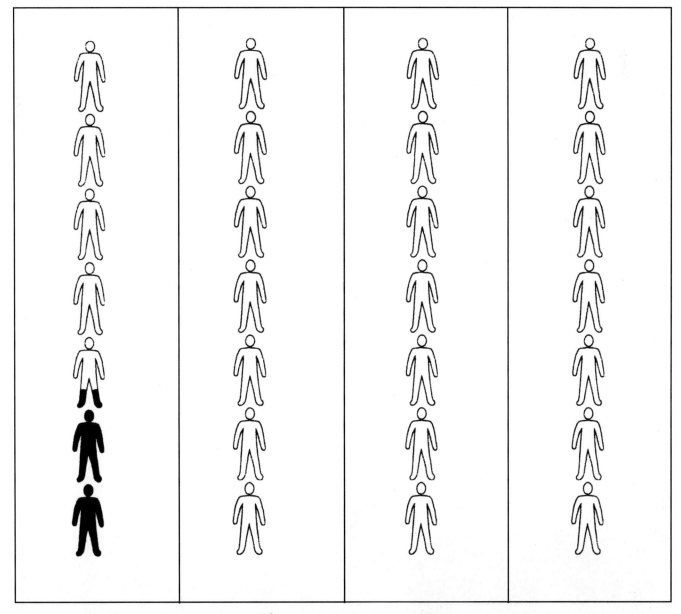

| 1841 | 1861 | 1881 | 1901 |

Muddy streets made shopping hard, especially for women in their long skirts. The Victorians solved the problem of mud by making more and more of their roads from pebbles or blocks of stone. However, shopping could still be dirty and difficult. By the 1870s, most new houses had proper toilets but there were more and more horses fouling the streets. Cart-wheels sent filth everywhere, and the noise they made was deafening.

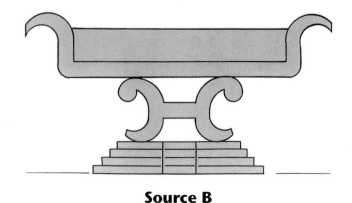

Source B

Victorian streets

Look at **Source B**.

Some people had one of these items outside their door. What do you think it was for? Why did they need it?

Source A

This is how Dickens described a morning scene in a London street:

Now and then a stage coach covered with mud rattled briskly by ... The public houses, with gas-lights burning inside, were already open ... Then came ... groups of labourers going to their work, then men and women with fish-baskets on their heads, donkey carts laden with vegetables, carts filled with livestock or ... meat, and milk-women with pails ... It was market morning. The ground was covered nearly ankle deep with filth ... , and a thick steam ... rising from ... the bodies of the cattle mixed with the fog, which seemed to rest upon the chimney tops ...

Source C   *Victorian shopping at its best.*

Victorian shops

The painting in **Source A** was done in 1898, 28 years after Charles Dickens' death.

1. Why do you think it differs so much from Dickens' description? (Try to think of more than one reason.)
2. Why do you think Victorian shops had signs as well as their names in words?
3. What sorts of places still have signs today?
4. Look at the passage by Charles Dickens. Why are there cattle, horses and donkeys in the streets?
5. Dickens mentions fog and chimneys. How do you think the two were connected?
6. Some of the people are going to market but one lot are going from house-to-house. Which people do you think they are? (Hint: we still have the same thing delivered today.)

Shopping

Look at **Source C**.

1. What kinds of toys are the shops selling?
2. Why would shopping be pleasant in this place?
3. What type of people could shop there?
4. Why do you think this picture was painted?

Source D *Reconstruction based on a Co-op grocery department.*

Shops were usually small, gloomy rooms in the owner's home. **Source D** shows a museum reconstruction of a grocer's shop. Most of the goods were in tubs or sacks, and the grocer used his scales to weigh what each customer wanted. Butter and sugar were in huge blocks; the grocer cut and shaped each customer's piece of butter with two wooden 'patters'; he sold the sugar in lumps which the customer had to break up.

Chemists' shops had shelves full of strange-looking packets and bottles. Often, the chemist had mixed these medicines up himself, using plants and chemicals. He put Latin names on the labels to make the medicines seem special. He also put big pointed bottles of coloured water in his windows. They helped to show which shop it was and they made it look strange and mysterious.

The chemist

Look at **Source E**.

1. What is the chemist doing?
2. Why do you think the chemist is dressed this way?
3. How is medicine stored?
4. Can you think of reasons why people would visit the chemist?
5. Is this a real Victorian chemist shop? Give reasons for your answers.

Source E

The grocer

Look at **Source D**.

1. How do you know this is not a real Victorian shop?
2. Make a list of the goods this shop sells. Tick those goods which are still sold today.
3. Museums often reconstruct the past by building shops and homes as they were in the past. How does this help us understand the past?
4. How could you find out if Victorian shops were really like this?
5. Make a chart which lists the similarities and differences between this Victorian shop and today. You could record it like this:

Victorian and Today's Grocers	
Same	**Different**
People bought coffee.	Weighed in Victorian days. In jars and packets today.

19 Food and Drink

What people ate depended on how well paid they were, and this was linked to the job they did.

In his famous Report, Chadwick gives us clues to the diet of different workers:

The weaver lives on very innutritious poor food, seldom eats meat;
Irishmen subsist chiefly on potatoes;
The collier [coal-miner] ... drinks too much ... and both he and his family partake of animal food every day.

The mill worker has tea, sugar, bread and butter night and morning; meat, and either bread or potatoes, with a pint of beer every day for his dinner.

Traders known as hucksters sold 'tea, coffee, sugar, butter, cheese, bacon ... and other articles to the working people in small quantities'. They charged a very high price and said that this was to make up for people failing to pay their bills. Some traders cheated the poor by selling them food that was stale. For example, they smeared fresh blood over meat that was going bad.

The Victorians had some clever ways of studying what different groups of people ate. For example, they found out the weight of cattle that were driven to a market, then they found out how many people lived in the area. In Manchester, there was enough fresh meat for everyone to have a helping each day. However, the meat was not shared fairly: most of it went to the better-paid workers; the poorer ones had to make do with salted meat like bacon.

Even when parents had enough money, they sometimes fed their children badly, since they did not know which foods were best. Doctors complained that children were being given 'bacon, fried meat and fatty potatoes when they had not, perhaps, two teeth in each jaw'. Parents also gave them drugs to send them to sleep; and some parents made themselves drunk in the evenings to forget their hard lives.

Diets improved as trains brought more and more fresh food into city centres. For example, Londoners started to eat Yorkshire rhubarb, and milk reached cities all over the country.

Source A

Victorian diet

Read the extracts from Chadwick's report and the child's diary.

1. Write a shopping list for each of the following:
   – a mill worker
   – a maid shopping for a well-off family.
2. Look at the photograph of the shop (**Source A**). How did traders cheat people?
3. What kind of shop is it?
4. How many people work there?
5. Why do you think the photograph was taken?
6. Make a list of the products you can see for sale.

Well-off people had meat, but this did not always keep them healthy. A Victorian child wrote in her diary:

At dinner time Papa gave Emily a choice piece of pheasant [wild bird] with bread sauce and potato, but she refused the pheasant ... so Papa took it to dear Leo ... It was the last thing he ate that he enjoyed.

Source B

Victorian cooking

Look at the picture of the cooking range (**Source B**).

1. How do you think the ovens were heated?
2. Where would bread have been baked?
3. How might meat have been cooked?
4. What do you think the chains and pulleys were used for?

55

A Family Budget

The Victorians divided a pound into 20 shillings (s). Each shilling was made up of 12 pence (d). In Victorian times, wages and prices were both far less than those of today. Each pound, shilling or penny was worth far more to the Victorians than it would be to us.

Source C

Expenditure for six people	£	s	d
Rent for two rooms		4	0
Bread and flour		5	4
Meat and suet		5	0
Butter and cheese		2	8
Tea, sugar and milk		2	4
Vegetables		2	0
Coal and wood		1	4
Candles, soap and so on.			9
Children's schooling		1	3
Sick club			9
Beer for the man at work		1	0
Beer at supper for man and wife		1	2
Tobacco			3
'Newsman'			1
Halfpenny for each child as a treat			2
Savings for clothing, breakages, doctor's fees and so on.		1	11
Total	**£1**	**10**	**00**

Victorian London

Source C shows what a Victorian family spent each week. (They lived in London in 1860.)

Using **Source C** to help you, complete the table below.

	My family	The Victorian family
Number of children		
Number of rooms		
Ways of keeping warm		
Ways of lighting gloomy rooms		
Main foods		
Pocket money		
Cost of schooling		
Payment to 'Newsman'		
Other things about the Victorian family		

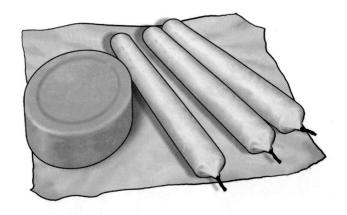

Children usually played in the streets, but for some who were free on a Saturday there was football on a local pitch.

Travelling shows were very popular. There were jugglers, fire-eaters and men with monkeys and dancing bears. There were also Punch and Judy shows in towns and on beaches.

People who went by train to the seaside often took a dip in the water. Men sometimes swam completely naked, but women changed in bathing machines. A bathing machine was a hut on wheels, and the woman could be wheeled right into the water to bathe in private.

Source A

At the seaside

Look at the photograph of the beach (**Source A**).

1. What time of year do you think it is?
2. What is the weather like?
3. Why are people using umbrellas?
4. How were the bathing machines moved in and out of the water?
5. List the activities people might do when visiting the seaside for a day.

Children played with simple toys like marbles, skipping ropes or tops.

Balls were too expensive to buy but sometimes they could make their own. One child explained:

In November came pig-killing time. Soon our ears would be tormented with the screams of the expiring [dying] pig; ... we hung round waiting for the bladder, which ... we blew up with a clay pipe stem.

Victorian games

Read this page and look carefully at **Source B**.

1. Use your own words to explain how some children made balls.
2. Is **Source B** a photograph of a 'real' Victorian room? How do you know?
3. How old does the teddy look? Do you think it belongs to the child in **Source B**? Give a reason for your answer.

Pleasures and activities

Look at **Source B** and read the extracts.

1. Make a list of all the toys and activities, putting one on each line. Now put a tick by any which we still have today, a cross by any we do not have, or a comment to say how things have changed. Perhaps your list will begin like this:

Toy or activity	Comment
Playing football	Victorian children sometimes made their own balls
Watching shows in the street	

2. How well off were the girls who went to the toy fair compared with other Victorian children? Why do you think so?

To spend an afternoon at the Winter Fair ... was like a visit to fairyland, because ... they entered from the gloomy street into a brightly gaslit interior... A brass band played lively marches, and the air was filled with a strong smell of wax dolls ... The smallest room ... contained toys ... for a penny. Whatever money came the girls' way during the year had to be saved for a spree in this room.

Source B

The Victorians were very interested in science. They liked to make use of what they learnt. Photography, electric lighting and the very first cars were all introduced during the Victorian years.

The Victorians were especially interested in light and how we see things.

Source A

Source B

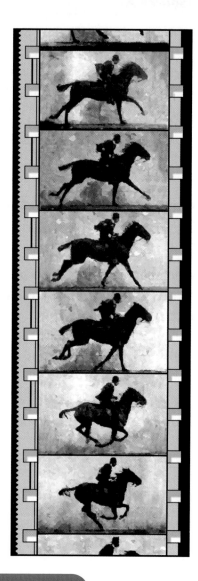

Moving pictures

Look at **Sources A** and **B**.

1. See if you can decide how the machine in **Source A** worked. The Victorians called it a zoetrope, or 'wheel of life'.
2. Films first appeared at the start of the 20th century, but they used discoveries made in Queen Victoria's reign. Look at **Source B** and try to explain how films work.

Flick books

Source C is a 'seeing toy' which the Victorians invented. To understand how it works, you can do a simple experiment.

1. Cut along the lines to turn **Source C** into seven strips.
2. Arrange them with number 1 at the top and number 7 at the bottom.
3. Hold them in one hand and flick the right-hand edges with the thumb of your other hand. If you look carefully you will see the flower grow. Perhaps you can make a better 'flick book' of your own.

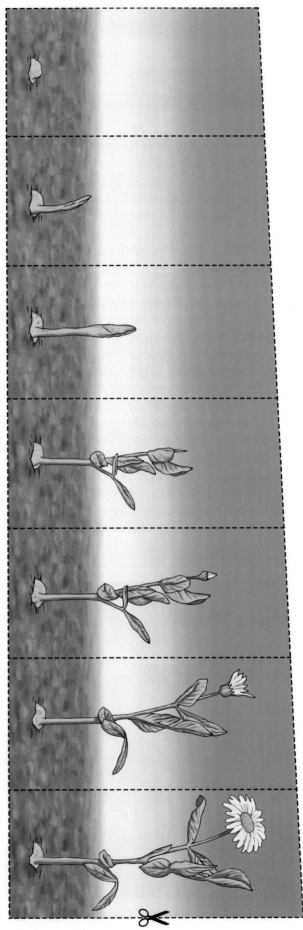

Source C

Front Page News

Pretend you are a newspaper editor working during Queen Victoria's reign. You have lots of news to fill your front page. Look at **Sources D**, **E**, **F**, **G** and **H** and choose four of them.

1. Think of good headlines and write the news reports.
2. Decide on a name for your newspaper. Design a heading to go across the top of the page.
3. Decide on the shape, size and layout of your front page and find a suitable sheet of paper. Mark with a pencil to show where everything should go.
4. Copy your reports onto the page. Take special care with your lettering and writing (you could use a computer).
5. Compare your newspaper with others in the class and see how they differ in what they say. (Real newspapers differ in just the same way.)

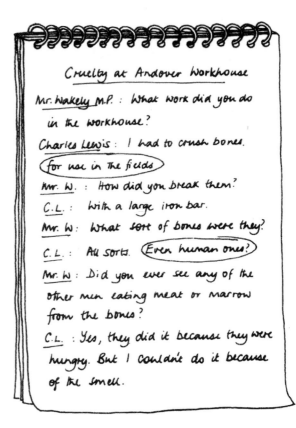

Cruelty at Andover Workhouse

Mr. Wakely M.P. : What work did you do in the workhouse?

Charles Lewis : I had to crush bones. (for use in the fields)

Mr. W. : How did you break them?

C.L. : With a large iron bar.

Mr. W : What sort of bones were they?

C.L. : All sorts. (Even human ones?)

Mr. W : Did you ever see any of the other men eating meat or marrow from the bones?

C.L. : Yes, they did it because they were hungry. But I couldn't do it because of the smell.

Source E *A reporter has brought you notes about an enquiry in the Houses of Parliament. His notes show what people said and he has added some extra points in rings.*

Source D *An artist has brought you a cartoon to show what happened to the doctors who have just invented something called chloroform.*

Science and Fun

"At the back of the whole row (on the north side of the street) there runs a series of little gardens, each house possessing one, in width equal to the frontage of the house it belongs to, and in length 56 feet. To every five houses there is a pump; and at the bottom of each garden a double privy, answering for two houses, the cess-pool shallow, and open to the air; and to this nuisance many have added a pig-sty, and dung or rubbish heap. The inhabitants of this street are poor people, chiefly silk-weavers, and what are here called frame-work-knitters or stockingers.

Number of the House.	Name of the Family.	Number of Persons ill with Fever.	REMARKS.
No. 25	Langton	3	Children, all of whom recovered.
" 26	Dearn	4	Man and wife, the former died.
" 27	Bailey	1	Man, who recovered.
" 28	Nettleship	4	Three children, and subsequently their mother. The children, after many weeks, recovered, but the poor mother (who was pregnant), being much weakened by the fever, and long attendance upon her children, died soon afterwards in child-bed.
" 29	Curzon	5	First a lodger, named Elizabeth Sherwin, (recently confined) and her infant, both died. Then three of Curzon's children, who recovered.
" 30	Hatfield	1	A girl, who recovered.

Source F *You have a copy of a huge new book by Edwin Chadwick. This is part of what it says about dirt and disease in the city of Leeds.*

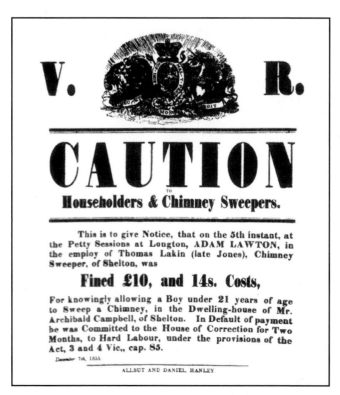

Source G *You see this poster outside your office.*

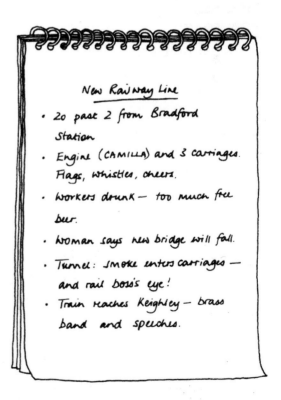

Source H *A reporter has brought you some notes about the opening of a new railway.*

Index